Vermont My Home

on

Blue Heron Pond

a love song for the earth

Dedicated

to

you

who are fearlessly tender in your

courage, care and love to create

a more sane peaceful

world

Vermont Art Poetry Press: 773 Guilford Street Brattleboro, Vermont, Individual prints, CDs and books can also be ordered at: www.vermontpoetry.com.

Profits from this book are donated to GRACE Cares a not-for-profit organization that supports community development programs throughout the world www.gracecares.org

Copyright © 2024 by Namaya

All rights reserved. No part of this book may be reproduced or transmitted in any form or by any means without permission by the author.

Cover photos by Namaya. Book design with Nookie Rivera.

Review:

"I enjoyed Blue Heron Pond very much. The fact that nature is central to the collection adds to its peaceful, meditative, spiritual quality. The book reaches a lovely place. Thank you."
Janisse Ray author of <u>Ecology of a Cracker Childhood</u>

TABLE OF CONTENTS

Love Song for the Earth.. 5
At the Center of the Universe 6
Am I Worthy?... 7
Home 8
Eternal Summer 9
Li Pon on Clouds and Love: Love is love 10
Tender in our love 11
Midnight in the Pond 12
As Rain Winds its Way Into the Intimate Sanctuary
Where Stones Dream 13
Swimming to the Higher Ground 14
Fire Inspires Memory... 15
Great Quiet Joy.. 16
Infinity of Love Redux 17
Revelation 18
Peak Colors Vermont 19
October Reminder 20
February Lion in Wait 21
Bliss.. 22
Snow held captive to our dreams 23
Angels' Joy 24
Our Grandparent's Farm 25

Snow's Feral Enchantment 28

Harvest 29

Buddha Sits: Dharma Blue Heron Pond 30

Ice Skating with Li Pon 31

Good Rain of Irene 32

Sunday Morning Joy 34

Sunlight Blissful 35

January Barren 36

The Unexpected Geometry of Perfection 37

Keep the Home Fires Burning 38

Red Barn Peeking through Snowy Woods 39

As Rain Wind Its Way Into The Intimate Sanctuary
Where Stones Dream: 40

Empire 41

Urgent Love 42

Betrayal 43

Neighbors 44

Value of Home 46

Hello 47

The Well Trod Path 48

Blue Jay Poseur & Blue Heron Diva 49

Basho & I on Blue Heron 50

Regrets 51

Suttee 52

Yellow Finch's World 53

Zin Pond Vermont 54

Home 57

Vermont 58

CARE WELL 60

About the author
Namaya 62

LOVE SONG FOR THE EARTH

Welcome, let's walk by Blue Heron Pond and these sacred woods.

In these stories and poems, I've spoken of life around this pond, of the foxes, beavers, deer, and every so often, black bears who amble down from the hills; the dozens of birds who make their home here; the flowers and plants who sing to each other even in their slumbering winter dreams: this is the microcosm of heaven—water, life, abundance and peace. The serenity of the pond from season to season and the simple meditation of waking up each day and writing poems about it is the great joy that fills my spirit. Some days are spent not even writing, just sitting here watching life unfold and being astonished.

These poems and stories are windows to the sublime joy when imagination and reality blend. Voila! The monk Li Pon makes his debut at Blue Heron Pond and, by the way, he told me that he appreciates you're part of his world.

I grieve for the violence and pain on the planet and offer these poems as - prayers for healing, a love song for Gaia, great mother Earth who has offered us heaven on earth. How do we nurture and revere this heaven? The Blue Heron of this pond –she is the spirit guide and muse who graces these waters and blesses our journey. We are caretakers of this sacred garden.

Come, let's take a walk by the shores of Blue Heron Pond.

At the Center of the Universe

blue
heron
pond

stillness
at
the
center
of
the
universe

Am I Worthy?

I'm surrounded
by a dense forest
of towering hemlocks

to the west,
birch and maple
to the south and

a rotting oak
struck by lightening
stands by the pond's edge.

When I first came here,
out of breath from NYC,
I walked through thick
underbrush to the pond,
barely visible from the hill.
I stood out there with
the Real Estate agent,
as if a dollar or a million
dollars could purchase
any of this. An abandoned
beavers' house was by the
far shore. From the northwest
a great blue heron
slowly soared across
the cattails, effortless
landed atop
the beavers' house
and turned to look
at me directly. Not
in an idle scan of
her surrounding, but
a look that seemed to
weigh and measure
my worth as her
neighbor on this pond.

Home

I've climbed the Himalayas and
Andes, sailed down the Amazon,
kayaked in the fjords of New
Zealand, visited Angkor Wat journeyed to the
Taj Mahal, south to Machu Picchu,
nights in the serenity of the Sahara, and
for a time at home in Yemen and Morocco.
Traveled Paris to Moscow, China, hundreds of
cities or more, across Ladakh and Kashmir;
the world well known, but like
all true travelers, I admit, I've barely
seen much of the world. Though
it is with exquisite pleasure I've seen
and tasted so much, there is an
unparalleled bliss of being here at home
in these green Vermont mountains
which open like welcoming arms that
cradle and envelop me--a babe held
to the breast.

Eternal Summer

High summer in Vermont,
trees are a thick collage
of green as far as the eye can
see... stout plump firs,
shaggy hemlocks,
virile oaks, and
maples dreaming of
flaunting their flaming
red and orange leaves.

Purple cone flowers,
succulent yellow
coltsfoot, red bee balm
that invites
the hummingbirds,
tiger lilies
voluptuous
in orange and
lavender irises
are summer's bouquet.

By the green murky pond
a bower of willows
lean together and their
supple tendril fingers
meet like folded hands
in prayer. I float on
my back, arms spread
wide, adrift, as the
pearlescent clouds and
the pale indigo sky
parts wide. I am a

seed floating
inconsequentially on
the water, more thoroughly
anointed than John the Baptist.

Li Pon on Clouds and Love: Love is love

Sky clear
not even
a trace
of a cloud,

a thread,
or a single
filament
of doubt,

as Li Pon
elegant
calligrapher

writes
with his
finger
to the
heavens,

like a
skywriter with
a biplane,

*Love
is
Love.*

It hovers above
Blue Heron
Pond like
a blessing
and the south
spun wind
takes it round
the world.

*Love
is
Love.*

Tender in our love

needing
to
be
far
more
tender
in
our
love
for
the
world
&
our
selves.

Midnight in the Pond

July in Vermont swimming naked at midnight in our pond, the moon a slender silver arc, stars strewn casually across the sky, we backstroke across the luminescent waters and gaze lovingly at our private planetarium. A sudden cold spring in the middle, then a bit of warmth, our feet sink in the primal ooze and we wade to shore, lying on the grass, drying ourselves in the sultry breeze -- our waking reveries entwined with the night.

As Rain Winds its Way Into the
Intimate Sanctuary Where Stones Dream

Lovers.

I am facing this stone wall.

Rain splatters against it:

The ashen belly of the sky is
brooding and swollen.

In the split cracked moment when
thunder cleaves
and the deluge comes

the August sky
bursts

and the stone wall
listens

to the pulse of rain and molecules of
stone
disintegrate
inside one
another.

Lovers.

Swimming to the Higher Ground

Wading into the squishy
ooze of the pond and
sinking like a granite boulder.

Legs are immobilized by the
turgid mud, ensnared
in the mire of fear.

Piranhas and alligators swim
patiently nearby, ready to feast.

It causes them to thrash excitedly.

Do I surrender to fear? To
the certainty of death?

I take all my doubts and fears
roll them into a big ball of bait
and toss it into the middle of their
ravenous desires.

I lie back and languidly backstroke
to shore, savoring the vivid cobalt blue
sky and the bracing chill of September.

Fire Inspires Memory

Do you remember
the full moon in
late August how
she painted the
sky with luminous
fire, kissed the
waters with her
passion and
incited the night's
chorus to an
orgiastic reverie?

I remember well
the moon on that
night and making
love with you, as
if time itself had
paused and we
were on an island
swaying in a
hammock spun
from our private
tender loving.

How does the
reverie of sun
hold through
the night?

How does the
enchantment
of night hold
us fast to
dreaming?

Great Quiet Joy

snow
envelops

hush

snow
deep

falling
rush

snow
sleep

dreams
to keep

Infinity of Love Redux

shrouded
in
mist

pond
elusive

desires
infinite

Slow Joy

slow joy
savored

kicking
autumn
leaves

swirls
of
gold

Revelation

I needed the
emptiness
to open
wide
and
wash
over
me.

The teacup,
porcelain with
a faded pink blossom,

was left on the
porch table and
the rain fell for
the entire afternoon.

Peak Colors Vermont

Succulently
vibrant

as if the red
could not
even contain
one more drop
of color.

Magenta
vibrant as
new lovers'
first kiss.

Sumac's
voluptuous
yellow so
alluring
the lemon
trees in
Seville
gave a
jealous
shudder.

Love is
longing
and fire.

October Reminder

October blows in with its windy bluster, tempting hints of sun, invitations of gold and red, and inundations of rain. All reminders -- gather wood, clean the furnace and stove, turn off the outside faucets, mend the roof -- seal and patch the cracks, store extra water and food, new candles, stock up on kerosene and lamp oil, the hundred score things that still need to be done, but the task most important--

is to hold every ounce of memory of the full summer sun as it warms my soul.

February Lion in Wait

February shouts in her
lioness roar
as she lies
in wait.

She purrs,

then snarls and spits,
takes a savage nip
from the rump of
Spring who has
just leaped past
my window

The lioness
lies in wait
patient to pounce
on the leaping
promise of Spring.

Bliss

eyes
lightened

blissful

sugar
snow

iridescent

brushes
across

tree
tops

Snow held captive to our dreams

nascent
dreaming winter flight of snow

whirling
spun by caprice

in the chastity of a chalice full
of dreams

the world spins in flight
soaring sightless

breathless in its haste to
   home

Angels' Joy

cold night
step outside
a glass of
bourbon
on the porch

snow flakes
fall and drift
a few land in
the glass
better than
ice and

the dregs
remain

the bourbon
warms

evaporates
to heaven

angels
smile

Our Grandparent's Farm

Out on the back roads of
Guilford heading towards
Vernon is the old family farm
now abandoned.

A farm is a cycle of
seasons, sorrows, and
harvest unbroken
through time.

I spent the afternoon walking
around the pastures, fields,
and corn silos. The barn
still smelled like cows.
I saw the ghosts
of men, women, and children
who had worked this
land for more than a
hundred and fifty years.

Fields, boulders, and tree stumps
leveled out as best as possible,
enough for hayfields and pastures
cleared by a team of horses and men.

Vermont farms are
flinty stone-filled farms
that reluctantly offer a
harvest. It is unrelenting
brutal work, from the heat of
the summer when
the stench and heat of the barn almost
knocks you over,
to the bitterly cold January
nights where the temperature
slips way below zero.

Grandpa' who never
complained -- said,
"Yup, cold tonight."
Yet, each day at 4 am, he was up and
heading to the barn. It was
like watching a sailor walk
on a ship as he ambled out
on arthritic hips and knees
that could barely hold him
up, but he could still swing
a 10-gallon milk can as easily
as a man decades younger.
365 days of the year, morning
and evening milking without respite.

Grandma was the spine,
the spirit and grit
who held our farm and
family together.
When there was little,
she made do. When there
was extra, she stored it.
She was ten farmhands
in one strong woman,

stubborn in her
unyielding love.

When our grandparents
passed away, no one wanted
to take over the farm, all the
kids who grew up on it said,
"Much too hard,
and doesn't make a bit of sense."

Farming is a stubborn love,
in the freezing snows,
the uncertain promise of spring,
and at last the harvest.

A single cow, a big Holstein
ready to be milked,
probably from a neighbor,
was grazing on the upper
pasture in a field of
daisies framed against an
azure blue sky and
looked at me
as if

I knew the fate
of our farm.

Snow's Feral Enchantment

winter turns in for
the final sleep

hushed in the womb of
her own being

snow drifts in ghosted
incantations

stalks the memory of
memory itself

Harvest

Pumpkin season sky
    unfurls like a clean fresh sheet:
palest of blue --
    single song note of a flute.

Attention is riveted
    by the leaf burnt, apple ripe,
tart sensation of the wind.

What whispered voice memory
    of fire
compels the virile, succulent
    green to surrender?

What wind spun incantation invites
    the fall
and shouts down the
    fortressed and sheltering leaves?

Why has the root's driven thirst
    for the sun surrendered
to the shivering naked limbs?

Why does the pumpkin season sky
    bleed
into the sullen leafed earth?

And how has the moon spoken
    to your ancient soul?

Buddha Sits:
Dharma Blue Heron Pond

Rock 1

rock
sits
ever
patient
waiting

for
blue
heron

Rock 2

rock
sits
patient

for

blue
heron

Rock 3

Buddha
blue
heron
pond

Rock 4

Buddha
is
rock.

Buddha
is
blue
heron.

Buddha
is
pond.

Rock 5

Li Pon
says--

"Rock
off.

Rock
on!"

Ice Skating with Li Pon

Li Pon gliding
across the pond

big figure eights,
even a pirouette
or two, monk's

saffron robes
swirl in a billowing
cloud; sunlight
bright against
the sullen green
hemlocks.

It was an ideal
day for ice
skating…

except –

it was a warm
Spring day in
December.

"Li Pon, there
is no ice in the pond!"

The words
reverberated
and in mid flight
he looked at me

puzzled,

"No ice?"

He leaped high,
but was drawn
to the sure gravity
of the earth.

Ever so lightly
his feet touched the

pond as he skated to
the north and then

… sailed
   upwards across the
      waving fingers of
         ferns and hemlocks.

"Don't be so attached
   to reality!" he called back.

Good Rain of Irene

The good rains of
    Irene fell today.

The winds shrieked and
    oceans of rain
fell across Vermont

Windows rattled and
    doors threatened to
bust open.

Debris swept
    through the streets,
houses and cars
    carried away by the flood.

Radio and television
    inundated us with
the news of the impending
    apocalypse

…as the good rain
    fell.

The good rain fell

not gentle
nor kind

not in goodness
nor tenderness

but in the telling
of the tale.

Rains swept
    aside fences
and washed over
    stone walls.

Rivalries, jealousies,
mistrust, old arguments,
feuds and misunderstandings

washed away in the torrent

…as the good rain
    fell.

The electricity was out
    for days and
homes torn
    away from their
foundations.

Neighbors and strangers
    came together.

Our homes opened for
    the homeless as
we shared meals
    by candlelight.
Musicians played
    at the Red Cross.

A thousand acts
and more of
kindness and
charity during
and after the storm

… as the good rain
    fell.

Sunday Morning Joy

Sunday morning joy

  warm luscious winds

    blowing in

      from the tropics.

Winds ripples

  across Blue Heron Pond.

    her hair blows

      in the wind.

Sunlight Blissful

Blue
   Heron
     Pond

expectations

dissolve

January Barren

Vermont in January
is wading through
dense banks of
snow, skiing,
sledding and snow
filled fun, but
in 2007 with
the topic of
global warming
burning on many
people's lips – nary
a peep of snow nor
even a taunting
whispery cloud
appeared.

The talk of global
demise is imminent…

till February turned
the corner, the air
became a bit moister,
and as the temperature
dropped

snow began to
  fall
    like the soft treading
      steps of a stalking cat
        through the tall grass.

The Unexpected Geometry of Perfection

Blue Heron on
the white rock
preens on her perch.

She is artistry in angles,
head pointing downwards,
body dropping backwards,
a step and turn as she looks
hungrily at the waters,
attentive to each ripple
and shift of the wind.

A turn and there is
another impossible
geometric form,
an angle of the beak,
flexing of the leg
and it is three
isosceles triangles
configured, her body
fluidly making
angles by a turn
of the head or step.
Picasso at his most
quintessential cubism,
would have been jealous.

I want to capture her
-- with my camera --
as I approach stealthily
the slight crack of a branch

some fifty yards away
startles her and with
her billowing wings
she strokes the wind
and is gone.

The unexpected
geometry of perfection.

Keep the Home Fires Burning

Temperature dropped way
down below freezing.

Sparrows tucked into
tree hollows, blue heron
nestled tightly into the
hemlock grove, and I'm
snuggled next to the fireplace.

And Li Pon?

I'm expecting him to
shake off his winter
slumber blues, throw
his thick woolen
robes to the ground
and ice skate across
the pond up to the
trees, but he and
Wu Ji, his winter
lover, are cozy in
their tiny yurt with
a trace of white smoke
curling up to the heavens
while their hut gently
rocks like a paper boat
on a stream—
    merrily,
        merrily.

Life is…

Red Barn Peeking through Snowy Woods

Red barn
recessed
   in
winter
woods.

Hint of red
peeking
demurely
through
collage
of
hemlock
ferns

snow

and

barren

oaks.

As Rain Wind Its Way Into The Intimate Sanctuary Where Stones Dream:

Lovers

The ashen belly of the sky is brooding and swollen

In the split cracked moment when thunder cleaves
and the deluge comes

the August sky
bursts

and the stone wall
listens

to the pulse of rain and molecules of stone
disintegrate
inside one
another

lovers

Empire

skies

  call

    violet

serene

  melody

    tranquility

  with

    every

indigo

  note

    blown

  on

    the

wind

Urgent Love

Spring was impatient
   this year to be Spring.
Spring was thirsty
   NOW
      to be Spring.

Famished for the sun
   and lonely in her desire,
she awoke one morning
stretched her arms wide
   in a yowling urgent
yawn of excitation.

Called back the geese!
Raised the robins to sing!
Frogs to shout their love!
Crocuses to thrill again!
Tulips to drink the colors
   from the sun itself!

Spring was impatient
   this year to be Spring.

Betrayal

snow in
Vermont
after the
crocuses
have
bloomed

with their
purple
and sun soaked
yellow
exclamation --

Spring!

Neighbors

*Neighbors from the
old English word
"near farm."*

Last night our neighbors
came by for a potluck supper
on the back porch
of our home at Blue Heron Pond.
Breaking bread and
sharing supper
is a tradition as old
as tribe and family.
Last week my neighbor
started to chain-saw
at seven thirty in the morning.
Though I am awake by six a.m.,
I like my morning quiet.
"Damn!" I thought. Then on
second thought. "Maybe
he needs help?"
But there are no
hard words between us.
We talked and found
a compromise.
Not his way nor mine,
but ours.
It is not our differences that
define us, but more of the
well trod path between our
homes.
We are neighbors, a kinship
born from a sharing of the land

and enduring
friendship that is closer than kin.
A tree falls in the driveway
and we work
together with chainsaws pulling
it out of the way.
A tool that is needed
is easily found in their shed
or ours. If my tall ladder is
missing it's being used next door.
When our neighbor's dad was
ill we helped care for
their elderly father. When
Pops passed away we
helped to carry the casket
and mourned together.
We are neighbors born of
celebration and caring.
A kinship born from a shared love
of the land, through floods
and storms, and even through
our infrequent disagreements.
We are bound together in the
enduring web of community
and neighbors.

Value of Home

Real Estate agent started to spin out some mighty
   big dollars for my home.
I felt like I had won the lottery!

"That much?"

"And you'd never need to work again.
   This is Fat City, boy."

"What will happen to my home and this land?"

"Rip down the old shack! The future is
   condominiums!" The words rolled
easily off his tongue. "But of course we would
make it classy to optimize the aesthetic value." he said with a wide smile.

"Optimize the aesthetic value? What the hell does that mean?"

"Boy, that means lots of green backs." he said while pushing a contract
   and a pen forward.
"Make your dream come true and sign on the line!"

I looked out at the woods, this tiny corner of heaven--
   the pastures of cowslip, clover, and rye by the pond's edge; the
way that sun light mirrors the hemlocks in the pond; the blissful
   thrill as the wind brushes across the tree tops.

I knew the worth and pushed the paper back to him.

   "Double!" he shouted.

"No. More worth and value to this land,
   than even you can begin to measure." I finally said.

Hello

excited to
see Blue
Heron Pond.

Two long
weeks on
the road,

trees bare

tattered
brown leaves
clatter in
the wind.

I've missed
Li Pon and
the monastery crew.

Will they
rush to
greet me?

"Hello, anyone home?"

The Well Trod Path

I've spent my life taking
the path least familiar and
less traveled on five
continents, but a path
that is best cherished is
the well-trod one through
the woods to my neighbor's house.
About a hundred yards or
more, whether in the summer
or any season, the path winds
through the woods to their
backdoor. I generally don't
knock, but give a call of
"hello" and most times it is
a call back of, "Come on in."
A glass of water or wine is offered,
and if it's around dinner, an extra
plate appears on the table.
If a tool is needed it's there
in their shed or ours, readily
available.
This well-trod path through the
woods so familiar and known
that even in the pitch black of
night we can find our way to each
other's door.

Blue Jay Poseur & Blue Heron Diva

Blue jay came whipping
across the pond shouting
'This is my pond!'

Starlings, woodpeckers,
sparrows, deer and
the hundreds of other
beings who live by
this pond, including this
poet, know we are merely
supporting cast to the
diva Blue Heron;

as if on cue, she soars
across the cattail marsh
and lands on the white
rock as the blue jay
vanishes.

Basho & I on Blue Heron

Old friend Basho
and I are looking
at the pond again.

He raps out
a beat in
5
7
5.

Words
dance

leap

on
blue
heron
pond.

bipi di
bop.

Rascal poet, Basho!

Regrets

there are regrets in my life--

missed meetings and chances,
fortunes that could have been
gained, money squandered, but

the regret that haunts me the most
is that I did not spend enough time --

gazing idly at the moon.

Suttee

watch the leaves
creating a poem

the slow pirouette
of fire and dying

ecstasy to love.

revelation
burning
into
desire.

love.

redemption.

fire.

Yellow Finch's World

yellow finch
lands on my
porch railing

some eight
feet in front
of me and
peers at me
through the
window.

she looks at
me, almost
startled as
if to ask,

"How did you get in my world?"

Zin Pond Vermont

Josiah, my neighbor, was talking to me
one day and said, "Yup, I can make your
piss piddle of a pond a mite bit bigger."
   Yup, I can."

Josiah got himself a big damn bulldozer
and almost dug out my pond right down
to the hardpan. Almost! The rains came
for a week, my pond flooded, and the dozer
bogged down like a dinosaur in the La Brea
     tar pit
"Don't worry. Sure 'nuf, we'll get that son of a bitch
     out of the hole!"

Next day up my driveway I heard
a noise so fierce I thought it was
an army invasion. It was a the
largest 18 wheeler I'd ever seen.
that was hauling the most
monstrous of dozers you could imagine.

Once he got this lumbering beast down
the hill the earth was trembling and
he plucked that tiny dozer out of the
pond as easy as you would suck marrow
out of a bone.

This was a premier dozer, like a
a prehistoric brontosaurus,
when the gears would grind -- flocks
of birds would fly up and the trees
would shudder as it dropped its head

to devour a huge bite of pond muck
and weeds streamed from its steely jaws,
"Chomp! Chomp! Chomp!"

   Josiah was looking gleeful maniacal
      in the saddle pulling back on the
levers like he was holding the reins for a team
      of oxen as he flogged that beast
and late into night we heard
      him yelling, "Ya' upp, get up on up thar'
      mangy good fer nuthin' sons of bitch!"

It was a wee bit hard to understand him at times,
but I had discovered as a Vermont farm boy descended from
      generations of farmers from the
the Green Mountains, English wasn't his first language.

No, sir, indeed. It was Vermont, pure and as thick as the
      first run of maple syrup! With a bit of a peculiar twang
from just over the Guilford line, but a "Y'up" is
      well understood in these parts, but Josiah was always
a mite bit hard to understand with his toothless grin and his
      one lone tooth standing on
the lower gum like a brown sentinel. Getting creamed with
      a few falling trees over the years also left his linguistic
abilities a mite bit peculiar. So I went and talked to his wife Mabel.

Mabel is a lovely butterball of a Vermont
      farm wife and when I asked her if she had any
trouble understanding him, she said, 'Ah Nup,' but he ain't
      said nuthin' in yars' far as I can tell. He just mumbles
and if it's morning, noon or six o'clock I put food on the table and he
      stops mumbling. If it's Sunday after church and he's
mumbling real loud I give him some lovin' and
      he falls asleep for the afternoon and I got out to the race track. No, sir
I don't have any problem understandin' him."

I fell asleep that night and in my dreams I kept hearing the
   voracious hungry roar of the dozer, after awhile
it was soothing like how Jonah must have felt in
   the grumbling growling belly of the whale.

Somewhere in the wee early dawn before sunlight crept
   over the hemlocks I heard a god awful yowl.
      "Let 'er rip ya' sons of bitch!"

Then for the next few hours I dozed back into that perfect
   lulling sleep one gets by the seashore. I felt I was back
in the primordial womb, but daylight wouldn't let me
   sleep one more minute. I turned on the coffee
maker, opened my eyes, and looked at the tiny quarter of an acre pond
   that was now about a good half mile wide and a mile or more long!
In the middle where the beaver lodge use to sit was a massive white
   boulder and Josiah sitting on my porch with a corncob pipe,
He smiled his toothless grin and spit a long stream of chew tobacco.

"Josiah," I said. "I asked you to scrape out the pond a little not make it
   into goddamn Lake Cuomo."
He looked at me funny, "Lake Cuomo? That thar' up by Montpelier?
   Look like one dam fine son of a bitch of a pond. Ya' up. Sure is. And I
     put that rock thar' – saw a picture in a magazine once of a Zin Pond."

"You mean Zen Pond?

"Yup, that thar' what I say, a Zin Pond. Make ya want to come back as a
   god damn frog in yar' next life!" He laughed so hard he choked
another stream of chewing tobacco spit flew out of his mouth. "Damn
   fine son bitch of a pond."

I looked at the spot where my tiny pond once was and now replaced
by one of the largest lakes in Southern Vermont and a massive white
   boulder in the middle.
A great blue heron rose from among the hemlocks circled once around
   and landed lightly on that rock and looked at both of us.

I looked at Josiah and said, "Yup, that thar's one fine son of a bitch of a
   Zin pond."

Home

I love the seasons as they
unravel and come to splendor.

I love the pace that we
live, busy but not too busy.

I travel around the world,
live many different lives,

but my compass points direct,
always to these mountains

where my soul finds comfort

Vermont

Native born or recent flatlander
two hundred years or two hundred
days, these mountains with their
million year history could care less.
We're all strangers to the land,
at best an estranged and alien species,
a foreign born virus swept in on
an ill wind, that will root and wither.

I may offer names for trees
or flowers, as if I knew their secret,
true nature --as if I knew of
what they dreamed or
anything at all of this land.

Gouged on the surface for ski
trails; granite and marble quarried
for our impermanent monuments;
rock filled soil that begrudgingly
offers a harvest; factories and sewage
that belch progress and effluence,
and nuclear power plants with their
sarcophagus of technology.

When I listen to the wind,
how it brushes across fields
of black-eyed daises and violets;
when I hear the exultation
of sunflowers in their sun
thirsty adulation to the day;
when I plunge into the
cold mountain streams –

Will this bring me home?

When will I revere this
earth, holier than any church,
as sacred as the Ganges when
the first molecule of water was
spoken, and precious and holy,
simply because it is-- the earth.

I lay claim to the land--
vivisect, bisect, and inspect
its value down to the last cent,
but hold no respect for its
true worth. How does one weigh
or measure a miracle? In a
handful of soil, that I crush
underfoot without thought,
lies the alchemy of life.

In this green, green oasis --
I am thirsty and famished
in pursuit of the hour.
Lonely and fearful
in my desire to love.

I too easily forget what is
most important to love:
the air, earth, this land,
water and the hour.

CARE WELL

Blue Heron Pond –

sacred body of water
has taught me more
of reverence than any church,

wiser in its quiet wisdom,
than any holy book or tome.
   Care well.
   It seems to say.
   Care well.

Swimming in the freezing
waters, ice cold springs
surprise and awaken me!

Finches, darts of yellow,
race across the fields.
Blue jay's screech warns!
   Care well!
   He seems to say.
   Care well!

Frogs' night chorus more
joyous and godly than any
Bach chorale. Tulips divine
the intersect of mystery,
revelation from the earth
and desire for the sun.

Blue Heron, sage of
this pond nests high
in the hemlocks,
is patiently biding her time.
> *Care well!*
> She seems to say.
> *Care well!*

In time we will all leave
this mortal sacred space,
but I will not grieve this end.

I will grieve if we have
not loved this earth with
sublime tenderness,
revered the waters as
dearly as our gods, cherished
the wisdom of a flower,
and held the divinity of
each living creature as a
mirror of god's love.

As god spun the planet
earth on her course and
brought it to life,

she set it free with this
single blessing:

> Care well.

NAMAYA

Namaya is a performance poet, and multimedia artist who has presented around the globe, and throughout his home state of Vermont. His creative work can be viewed at *www.namayaproductions.com*, *www.thejazzpoet.com*, and *www.vermontpoet.com*. Namaya has authored 2 plays "Beatnik Café: A Musical Revue of the Jazz Beat Generation," and "House of War: House of Glass" which is currently under production He is the author of God Sex Politics, Eros to Godhead, Celebrate Life: Viva La Vida, Thirst: A Novella of Redemption, and Journal of the Plague: Living and working with AIDS, and the children's story "On the Island of Binga Bonga." Namaya is currently working on a multiyear art and theater project on Agent Orange; to raise awareness of the continuing harm caused by this chemical used by the US military in Southeast during the Vietnam war.

Namaya is a co-founder of GRACE Cares, a not-for-profit organization that supports small scale community development and peace projects worldwide. A portion of profits from Namaya's writings and performances are donated to *www.gracecares.org* a not-for-profit organization that supports small scale community development and peace projects worldwide.

CD, music, stories, and photos of Vermont by Namaya can be ordered

And at the *www.vermontpoet.com/store*

photo credit Zoe Kopp